The Common Core Readiness Guide to Reading™

TIPS & TRICKS FOR

EVALUATING AN ARGUMENT AND ITS CLAIMS

Sandra K. Athans and Robin W. Parente

ROSEN
PUBLISHING®

New York

Published in 2015 by The Rosen Publishing Group, Inc.
29 East 21st Street, New York, NY 10010

Copyright 2015 by the Rosen Publishing Group, Inc.

First Edition

Library of Congress Cataloging-in-Publication Data

Athans, Sandra K., 1958–
Tips & tricks for evaluating an argument and its claims/Sandra K. Athans, Robin W. Parente.—First Edition.
     pages cm.—(The common core readiness guide to reading)
Includes bibliographical references and index.
Audience: Grades 7–12.
ISBN 978-1-4777-7559-2 (library bound)—ISBN 978-1-4777-7561-5 (pbk.)—
ISBN 978-1-4777-7562-2 (6-pack)
1. Debates and debating—Juvenile literature. 2. Persuasion (Rhetoric)—Juvenile literature.
3. Critical thinking—Juvenile literature. 4. Creative thinking—Juvenile literature. 5. Reasoning (Psychology)—Juvenile literature. I. Parente, Robin W. II. Title. III. Title: Tips and tricks for evaluating an argument and its claims.
PN4142.A85 2015
808'.03—dc23

                                                                2014006330

Manufactured in the United States of America

Contents

INTRODUCTION 4

CHAPTER 1: **A QUICK AND EASY OVERVIEW:**
THE SKILLS AND THE TIPS AND TRICKS 8

CHAPTER 2: **EVALUATING AN ARGUMENT**—ONE SIDE:
ANIMAL RIGHTS—EXPERT READER MODEL 15
    CLOSE READING 15
    MULTIPLE-CHOICE QUESTIONS. 20
    T-CHART 21

CHAPTER 3: **EVALUATING AN ARGUMENT**—THE OTHER SIDE:
ANIMAL RIGHTS—GUIDED PRACTICE 23
    CLOSE READING 23
    MULTIPLE-CHOICE QUESTIONS 28
    T-CHART 30

CHAPTER 4: **EVALUATING THE ARGUMENTS**—ANIMAL RIGHTS—
WRITTEN RESPONSE. 32

CHAPTER 5: **EVALUATING AN ARGUMENT**—ONE SIDE:
IMMIGRATION—EXPERT READER MODEL. 36
    CLOSE READING. 36
    MULTIPLE-CHOICE QUESTIONS 41
    T-CHART 43

CHAPTER 6: **EVALUATING AN ARGUMENT**—THE OTHER SIDE:
IMMIGRATION—GUIDED PRACTICE 45
    CLOSE READING. 45
    MULTIPLE-CHOICE QUESTIONS 50
    T-CHART 52

CHAPTER 7: **EVALUATING THE ARGUMENTS**—IMMIGRATION—
WRITTEN RESPONSE. 54

    GLOSSARY 57
    FOR MORE INFORMATION 58
    BIBLIOGRAPHY. 61
    INDEX 62

Introduction

The Common Core Reading Standards are a set of skills designed to prepare you for entering college or beginning your career. They're grouped into broad College and Career Readiness Anchor Standards, and they help you use reasoning and evidence in ways that will serve you well now and in the future.

The skills build from kindergarten to the twelfth grade. Grades six through eight take the spotlight here. You may already have noticed changes in your classrooms that are based on the standards—deeper-level reading, shorter passages, an emphasis on informational texts, or an overall increase in rigor within your daily activities.

This book will help you understand, practice, and independently apply the skills through easy-to-use "tips and tricks" in order to gain mastery.

The Common Core Standards were built upon the strengths and lessons of state standards as well as top-performing countries in order to prepare all students for success in a global economy and society.

Close Reading

Your teachers may use close reading for some of their instruction. During close reading you read shorter passages deeply in order to analyze them.

Close reading passages often have rich, complex content. They use grade-level vocabulary words, sentence structures, and literary techniques. Reading a short, three-page passage closely could take several days. The benefit to you is a deeper connection and comprehension of what you've read. Close reading is a critical part of the new Common Core Reading Standards and is used throughout this book.

Other reading comprehension skills such as visualizing, asking questions, synthesizing, and other traditional strategies work with the Common Core skills covered here.

This book focuses on Anchor Standard 8: Delineate and evaluate the argument and specific claims in a text, including the validity of the reasoning as well as the relevance and sufficiency of evidence. In the next chapter, we'll break these skills apart and look at them closely. Tips and tricks to help you gain mastery of this standard are introduced.

Guided Practice: How It Works

In the passages that follow, you tag along with expert readers as they think aloud while close reading from different informational texts (nonfiction). Unlike the other Anchor Standards, Standard 8 does *not* apply to literature. Argument is a specific kind of informational text not found in fictional works and literature. Although reserved for use with informational text, Standard 8 delineates skills that are nonetheless essential for the kind of critical reading and thinking this genre demands.

Visual icons that represent the tips and tricks appear in the margins and prompt the expert reader. Ways in which the expert reader applies them appear in expert reader margin notes. You'll also review multiple-choice questions, a method of organizing ideas in a T-chart, and a written response question completed by the experts. Explanations that support the expert reader's reasoning are provided.

After you understand how the skill is applied, it's your turn to try with guided practice. You'll apply the skill independently then perform a self-evaluation by checking your responses against answers provided. Based on your responses, you can determine if another pass through the expert reader's examples might be helpful or if you've mastered the skill.

CHAPTER 1

A QUICK AND EASY OVERVIEW: THE SKILLS AND THE TIPS AND TRICKS

Let's examine the skills needed to delineate and evaluate an argument and its claims. You've probably recognized that this standard is all about arguments. A written argument is a view or position that someone takes. It is supported by reasoning and claims. Claims are assertions or statements. To construct an argument in a written passage, text, or speech, an author does one main thing. He or she must present a series of logically organized reasons or claims. These are designed to persuade readers toward a belief, an attitude, or an action. Sometimes, the text or passage itself may be referred to as an argument. In well-supported arguments, an author will prove a point by using sound evidence that supports all of his or her claims.

The word "delineate" means to define or explain. This first step—to explain the argument—must precede the task of evaluating it. The word "evaluate" means to appraise or assess. So here we are going to learn and practice skills that help us appraise or assess arguments. The next part of this standard asks us to determine if the reasoning is valid, relevant, and sufficient. In other words, we need to gauge if the reasoning makes sense, if it is pertinent to the issue, and if it fulfills

Determining whether an author uses valid, relevant, and sufficient reasoning is a major part of assessing an argument.

the task of proof which the author intended. Determining the strength of an argument is critical. It affects your decisions, actions, beliefs, values, and more.

At times, you may need to make inferences about ideas or events not directly stated. It is equally important to monitor your inferences and consider whether or not they hold up to the same standards and criteria as the stated claims.

Text Analysis Tips and Tricks

There are several easy-to-use tips and tricks to evaluate an argument and its claims. Some are useful as you begin to read, while others guide you throughout your reading. The icons featured below are used in subsequent chapters to show you how the tips and tricks are used in action with informational texts.

● **Launching "Jump-Start" Clues:** Before you dive into reading a piece of text, scan it quickly. Take a visual inventory of everything you see. The title, subheadings, boldface print, and other features like photographs or charts will give you valuable clues about the content such as the topic of the argument, possible claims, or even the kind of support an author might include. Authors select titles carefully and use text features purposefully. It's often helpful to ask yourself: What could the title mean or what purpose do the special features serve? What will the author discuss and what angle might he or she take?

● **Using Text Structure (Flexibly) to Find the Central Idea or Argument and to Monitor its Development:** The central idea of a text passage typically emerges early on and then develops throughout the passage. The central idea may in fact be the author's argument. Distinguishing this may require careful attention to clues. Some ways an author could present an argument might be with an opinion statement, a quoted fact or facts, an anecdote, or other methods. As the argument unfolds, you will want to explore the author's use of claims and support. One way to do this is by monitoring the text structures. Authors organize ideas sequentially, using cause and effect, problem and solution, or multiple structures that help readers grasp, connect, and remember important information. Identifying these structures can help guide and validate your understanding of an argument and its claims.

● **Identifying and Monitoring Point of View or Perspective and Being Attentive to the Author:** As attentive and critical readers, we must examine an author's words and motives. Informational text is filtered through the author's perspective which means the information is subject to all of the views and beliefs held by the author. Knowing this is important as it enables us to determine biases or ways in which an author's line of reasoning may be influenced by their personal views and beliefs.

Determining the credibility of the author as a "knowledgeable" source is also essential. Authors of informational text establish their credibility by highlighting their personal or professional experience or through the quality of the claims they include in support of their argument. Being attentive to an author to detect biases and to gauge the quality of his or her claims is essential.

● **Using Craft and Text Structure:** Looking closely at how authors of informational text carefully construct and develop their ideas can help us gain a comprehensive understanding of their approach, their intentions, and the degree to which they have satisfied the burden of proof for their arguments and claims. Looking critically at smaller units of composition—such as sentences and paragraphs or lines and

Students are encouraged to read a text with care and use evidence to present careful analysis, defend interpretations, and support claims.

words—and explaining how they fit into the larger passage helps formulate this analysis.

● **Tune In to Your Inside Voice:** Your mind is actively making sense as you read. Listening to your thoughts or your mind's dialogue helps you grasp meaning. Connecting new ideas to known ideas is the way your

Quick Check Self-Evaluation for Evaluating an Argument and Its Claims

Determining how well you've mastered the tips and tricks for evaluating an argument and its claims is important. One way to do this is by gauging your success with the following tasks:

√ I can define the argument.

√ I've determined the reasoning and claims are **valid**.

√ I've determined the reasoning and claims are **relevant**.

√ I've determined the reasoning and claims are **sufficient**.

mind builds cohesive meaning. Monitoring your thoughts, including your questions, is critical. Does this make sense based on the evidence provided? Has the author sufficiently met the burden of proof?

 ● **Avoid Common Pitfalls:** Sometimes we can become distracted by something in the text, which could steer us away from an author's intended meaning. Staying engaged and focused while ensuring that your ideas square with text-based evidence is critical. In addition to this pitfall, there are others that you will want to safeguard against:

1. Emotionally charged topics may unleash your personal feelings and interfere with your ability to evaluate an author's claims. Although difficult, it's important to maintain focus on your evaluation of the author's argument and claims.

2. Weigh all claims and guard against being swayed in a direction too hastily. Evaluate all points in a line of argument by assessing how well each builds on the other. In a sense, readers must constantly consider the other side in order to critically investigate the author's position.

3. Carefully distinguish opinions and generalizations from facts. Authors may include their personal views as well as generalizations in an argument but must support them with facts.

As you practice and gain skill with these tips and tricks, you'll find that they work together and often become indistinguishable. This is a sure sign that they've become automatic and will kick in when they're needed.

CHAPTER 2

EVALUATING AN ARGUMENT—ONE SIDE: ANIMAL RIGHTS—EXPERT READER MODEL

In the following passage we will apply the tips and tricks for evaluating an argument and its claims. Read and follow the expert reader's thinking through a sampling of the tips and tricks in the margin notes. It's like tagging along with the expert reader.

The expert reader will then tackle some multiple-choice questions. This is followed by a quick self-evaluation of arguments, claims, and reasoning. These activities show how to apply these skills to informational text.

In the next chapter, it will be your turn to practice. Let's get started!

An Excerpt from:
Debating the Issues: Animal Rights
by Gail Mack

Animal rights is the idea that nonhuman animals are entitled to the possession of their own lives, and that their most basic interests,

EXPERT READER:

I notice several important items. The topic is animal rights, and there is a quick definition of the term. By scanning headings and subheadings, I see I'll be reading claims to support the argument that animals should not have rights. It looks like some of the reasoning will have to do with medical testing.

EXPERT READER:

The author uses phrases like "many people believe" several times and mentions that beliefs are based "on their opinion that animals are not enough like humans." My initial feeling is that she might feel animals should have rights. As I read, I'll be alert to how her reasoning for the argument might be influenced by her feelings.

I believe this first sentence delineates the argument: Animals are used for medical testing because it is necessary and benefits humans. As I continue reading, I will look for supporting claims that provide valid, relevant, and sufficient reasoning.

such as an interest in not suffering, should be afforded the same consideration as the similar interests of human beings.

One Side: Animals Should Not Have Rights

Many people do not believe that animals need or deserve legal rights. Their belief is based on their opinion that animals are not enough like humans. For example, do animals feel emotions? Human emotions include love, fear, joy, sadness, surprise, anxiety, and anger. People who believe that animals cannot feel emotions do not think they are entitled to legal rights. Although people often see human qualities in animals, regular scientific methods cannot prove that animals feel emotions. Many people believe that animals merely act—and react—according to their instincts and that they lack any ability to think and reason.

Medical Testing Using Animals

Animals are used for medical testing because it is necessary and benefits humans. The goal is to experiment with new medicines and vaccines first on animals to see how the medicines affect them before doing human studies. Animals used in experiments are usually euthanized afterward. Those that support using animals for experiments argue that nearly every twentieth-century medical achievement used animals in various ways. Supporters of animal use insist that computers cannot model the ways in which different things might interact during a test.

🛦 EXPERT READER:

Here are two claims to support the argument. 1) Nearly every twentieth-century medical achievement used animals in various ways, and 2) computers cannot model the ways different things might interact during a test. I'll continue reading to see if these claims can be supported with valid, relevant, and sufficient reasoning.

Polio is an infectious viral disease that attacks the nerve cells and sometimes the central nervous system. It usually causes paralysis and sometimes even death. Polio strikes mainly children, but adults can also be infected. In the 1940s, Dr. Jonas Salk used rhesus monkeys to isolate the three forms of the polio virus that affected hundreds of thousands yearly. Salk's team created a vaccine against the polio strains in the cultures of monkey kidney cells. This vaccine was made publicly

Dr. Jonas Salk (1914–1995) conducted medical research and testing on rhesus monkeys that resulted in the release of a polio vaccine in 1955.

EXPERT READER:

This paragraph helps develop the claim that nearly every twentieth-century medical achievement used animals in various ways by supplying facts about the polio virus and its vaccine developed using rhesus monkeys, adding that the vaccine virtually stamped out the disease in the United States within ten years. This reasoning seems valid, relevant, and sufficient and supports the claim and argument.

available in 1955 and reduced the number of polio cases fifteenfold in the United States over the next five years. Dr. Albert Sabin then made a superior "live" vaccine by passing the virus through animal hosts, including monkeys. His oral vaccine was produced for public use in 1963 and is still in use. It had virtually stamped out polio in the United States by 1965. An estimated 100,000 rhesus monkeys were killed in the course of developing these vaccines.

SARS

SARS (severe acute respiratory syndrome) is an illness that affects the lungs and breathing and can lead to pneumonia. It is caused by a SARS-related coronavirus. The first outbreak was reported in Asia in February 2003. Over the next few months, SARS spread to more than two dozen countries in North America, South America, Europe, and Asia before it was contained. The World Health Organization (WHO) has reported that 8,098 people worldwide became sick with SARS in the 2003 outbreak. Of these, 774 died.

EXPERT READER:

SARS sounds like a very fast-moving, dangerous illness for humans. It spread to two dozen countries on four continents within a few months.

Researchers found that a new coronavirus never seen in humans was the cause of SARS. When researchers infected monkeys with the new coronavirus, they developed a lung disease exactly the same as SARS. Ultimately, a SARS vaccine was developed. As of 2011, a federal health agency, the Centers for Disease Control

(CDC), was continuing to work with other federal agencies, state and local health departments, and other health care organizations to plan for rapid recognition of and response to the disease should it ever come back.

Protection for Lab Animals

Medical researchers study animals to learn about their body processes and how they relate to those of humans. Researchers also use animals to learn about the causes and effects of cancer, heart disease, and other illnesses. They also use animals to develop and test drugs, surgical methods, and safety standards in cosmetic and food products. Psychologists conduct experiments to study the effects of stress and hunger to learn how these conditions affect humans.

Today in the United States, researchers must follow certain federal and state laws and regulations. A federal law, the Animal Welfare Act of 1966, requires adequate food and shelter for certain kinds of lab animals. Each institution funded by the National Institute of Health must have a committee that oversees the use and care of the animals.

EXPERT READER:

This paragraph further develops the claim by using a problem/solution structure. It introduces SARS (problem) and the monkeys used to develop the vaccine (solution). This reasoning seems valid, relevant, and sufficient and supports the claim and argument.

The author provides nine additional claims that support the argument that medical testing of animals benefits humans. Although not as fully developed as the polio or SARS claims, they seem valid, relevant, and sufficient.

Although I'm wondering what happens to the animals that aren't considered "most animals" and what "adequate food and shelter" involves, I'll put my personal feelings aside since this will not help me further evaluate the author's argument and claims. I also notice that although I thought the author might be biased in her presentation of this side of the animal rights debate, she was not.

19

Mini Assessment

Now let's see how the expert reader grapples with some multiple-choice questions for this passage. Notice that in some cases more than one answer may initially seem correct. It is important to use evidence to identify the best answer. Carefully review the evidence by returning to the passage to gauge which response is best supported by the passage.

1. Why does the author include this sentence in the passage?
"In the 1940s, Dr. Jonas Salk used rhesus monkeys to isolate the three forms of the polio virus that affected hundreds of thousands yearly."

> a) To support her statement that "polio strikes mainly children, but adults can also be infected."
>
> b) To establish the fact that Dr. Jonas Salk created the first polio vaccine.
>
> c) To make sure readers understand the extent to which the polio virus affected human beings.
>
> d) To increase her believability as an expert on medical testing on animals.

2. Which sentence from the passage best supports the claim that "computers cannot model the ways different things might interact during a test"?

> a) "Those that support using animals for experiments argue that nearly every twentieth-century medical achievement used animals in various ways."
>
> b) "The goal is to experiment with new medicines and vaccines first on animals to see how the medicines affect them before doing human studies."
>
> c) "An estimated 100,000 rhesus monkeys were killed in the course of developing these vaccines."
>
> d) "Researchers found that a new coronavirus never seen in humans was the cause of SARS."

Check your answers. Were you correct?

1. c) is the best answer. This sentence helps the reader understand that since the development of the polio vaccine, hundreds of thousands of people every year have been spared from the devastating effects of the polio virus. Because of Dr. Salk's (and later Dr. Sabin's) experiments using animal hosts to create an effective vaccine, literally millions of people have not contracted the polio virus since 1965.

2. b) is the best answer. The key idea in the claim is that since computers are not living organisms, they can't possibly recreate how a medicine or vaccine might actually affect a person. The answer supports the claim that animals must be used because researchers can actually observe and notice the effect medicines and vaccines have on them and then decide if they're safe for people.

Expert Reader: I'm satisfied with my responses. In all cases I returned to the text and checked possible answers against the evidence. At times, I had to dig deeply into the text and use clues and inferences. I'm confident I can support my answers. Now, I'm ready to do a quick check self-evaluation using a T-chart. This will help me organize my ideas about the claims and decide if the reasoning is valid, relevant, and sufficient. I can then better evaluate the argument.

A Quick Check Self-Evaluation

Argument: Animals are used for medical testing because it is necessary and benefits humans.

Claim	Valid, Relevant, Sufficient Reasoning
Nearly every twentieth-century medical achievement used animals in various ways.	Polio has been nonexistent in the United States since 1965 because of vaccines developed through medical testing on monkeys. Before 1955, the polio virus affected hundreds of thousands of people a year. Polio vaccines potentially saved millions of lives.

	SARS was a quick-moving, dangerous coronavirus never seen in humans (2003). A vaccine was developed through medical testing on monkeys, and the outbreak was stopped.
Computers cannot model the ways different things might interact during a test.	Medicines, vaccines, surgical methods, cosmetics, and foods are tested on animals before humans to see how living things are affected by them. Computers cannot recreate an exact interaction because they are nonliving things. Doctors Salk and Sabin used monkeys to recreate the experience of a human contracting the polio virus and developed vaccines. Scientists developed the SARS vaccine because they used monkeys to replicate the exact lung disease humans were contracting.

Expert Reader: After evaluating my T-chart, I feel the argument is supported through a line of claims and reasoning. The reasoning is valid and makes sense. It is relevant to the issue of using animals for medical testing and sufficiently fulfills the necessary burden of proof. I'll revisit this chart in chapter 4 when I create a written response further evaluating the arguments in chapters 2 and 3.

Conclusion

How well do you feel you've grasped the expert reader's use of the tips and tricks for evaluating an argument and its claims? If you're ready, move on to the guided practice in the next chapter, or take another pass through the expert reader's model.

CHAPTER 3

EVALUATING AN ARGUMENT—THE OTHER SIDE: ANIMAL RIGHTS— GUIDED PRACTICE

N ow it's time for you to apply the tips and tricks during your close reading of a passage. The practice prompts icons will guide you although you may want to review the tips and tricks in chapter 1 for icon descriptors. Check to see if your responses to the prompts match the possible responses provided.

An Excerpt from:
Debating the Issues:
Animal Rights 🏃
by Gail Mack

The Other Side: Animals Should Have Rights

The field of studying animal emotions is part of the larger science called cognitive ethology (the

💻 GUIDED PRACTICE PROMPT:

🏃 How can jump-start clues help you? Possible response: A quick scan of the title, headings, and subheadings indicates that this passage will most likely present claims to support the position that animals should have rights. I'm thinking that some of the reasoning to support this argument will have to do with medical testing and research using animals.

study of animal minds). Research in animal emotions has grown and changed a lot over the last thirty years. Today most people who once wondered or doubted if animals could have emotions have discovered that animals do indeed have many of the same kinds of emotions that humans have.

There are six universal primary emotions that were identified by Charles Darwin, the first scientist to study animal emotions systematically. In 1872, he wrote that animals could feel fear, disgust, anger, surprise, sadness, and happiness. These emotions are produced in a part of the brain called the limbic system. Humans and many other species have limbic systems. 🔍

GUIDED PRACTICE PROMPT:

🔍 Can you identify the author's point of view or perspective? Possible response: The author gives the reader information on emotions and the limbic system to establish a common connection between humans and other animal species. By doing this, she might be hoping to persuade the reader to believe that humans are not that different from animals.

How can you use text structure to help establish the argument? Possible response: The author is using a question/answer format. She poses the question "Is medical testing necessary?" and then supplies claims to prompt a "no" response. The specific argument for this passage seems to be that animals should not be used for medical testing.

Is Medical Testing Necessary?

Animal rights advocates contend that medical testing that uses animals is needlessly cruel and old-fashioned and can cause much pain. They say medical testing on nonhuman species can produce misleading results and claim that changing the conditions that lead to a disease, not curing or preventing it, is probably better in the long run. 🪜 Money spent on experiments using animals could instead be spent on preventive measures that might save many more lives. In support of this view, they point out that in many cases researchers choose species less for their similarity to humans and more because they are cheaper and easier to work with and are in many instances familiar to laboratory staff.

Alternatives Research

A new option has slowly been developing: alternatives research. This is a search for replacements that will reduce the use of animals by means of a step-by-step process. Eventually, its supporters say, the process could lead to elimination of the need for animals. The Johns Hopkins Center for Alternatives to Animal Testing has received grants and gifts to sponsor research, and scientific interest in alternatives has produced legislative initiatives. First, however, researchers must find alternatives that work. The United States Food and Drug Administration (FDA) notes that many procedures that could replace animals are still in development. Ultimately, the FDA says, testing must progress to the use of an animal—not using animals for testing would put humans at unreasonable risk. The National Association for Biomedical Research (NABR) contends that in many areas of biologic and medical research, there are no substitutes for the study of living animals. The NABR says many processes in the human body are too complex for computers or cell cultures.

GUIDED PRACTICE PROMPT:

Have you noticed the author's craft and/or use of text structure? Possible response: Here are two claims to support the argument: 1) Money spent on experiments using animals could be better spent on preventive measures and 2) researchers only use animals because they are cheaper and easier to work with. Can these claims be supported by valid, relevant, and sufficient reasoning?

Can you use text structure to help identify claims? Possible response: The author uses a descriptive text structure to introduce another claim in support of the argument: Alternatives research could replace animals in medical testing.

How can you use text structure to explore support for a claim? Possible response: The descriptive structure provides valid, relevant, and sufficient reasoning to show that nonanimal research is not a viable option at this point and possibly at no future time according to the United States Food and Drug Administration (a reliable source, I believe) and the National Association for Biomedical Research (which sounds reliable, but I'd have to research more).

The Animal Rights Debate

In 1975, author Peter Singer called attention to the abuses of animals throughout the world in a book titled *Animal Liberation*. For Singer, the issue is not animal rights but animal equality. He charges that

Author Peter Singer challenged people to consider animal interests in his 1975 book, *Animal Liberation*.

humans are *speciesists*, or creatures who put the interests of their own species above those of other species. He says that in the past, most people did not believe that animals could suffer. They also believed animals had no interests and that humans, therefore, could not be guilty of neglecting their interests. The most important reason to consider animals' interests, he says, is that like humans, animals can and do suffer. On the other side of the argument are the scientists and others who believe that animal research and scientific testing are essential tools in the protection of humans from life-threatening diseases. In their view, animal research and testing are not inherently cruel. They hold to the traditional belief that "animal rights" as such do not exist; rather, that human beings have a moral obligation to treat animals with respect and to do them no harm beyond what is necessary to preserve and support human life. That is to say, people must treat animals humanely, even though sometimes the animals may have to endure pain and suffering from necessary laboratory experiments.

What do you think?

GUIDED PRACTICE PROMPT:

Are you noticing the author's craft and/or use of text structure? Possible response: Here is another claim to support the argument: Animals can and do suffer when they are used in medical testing. I can connect to earlier text explaining how Darwin identified fear, disgust, anger, surprise, sadness, and happiness as emotions that animals feel. Is this valid, relevant, and sufficient reasoning to support the claim?

What are you thinking? Possible response: This paragraph supports the paragraph that introduced the term "speciesists," creatures who put their interests above those of other species. Is this a bad thing?

What are you thinking? Possible response: After reading, I think I'll have to put aside two of the earlier claims I identified as I was unable to find valid, relevant, and sufficient reasoning to support them: 1) Money spent on experiments using animals could be better spent on preventative medicine and 2) researchers only use animals because they're cheaper and easier to work with. That's not to say there is not reasoning for these claims, but that reasoning was not included in this passage.

Mini Assessment

Remember that it's important to use evidence to build a case for the best answer. Return to the text to gauge which response is best supported.

1. Which claim from the passage is best supported by this sentence?
"In 1872, he [Charles Darwin] wrote that animals could feel the primary emotions: fear, disgust, anger, surprise, sadness, and happiness."

    a) Money spent on experiments using animals could be better spent on preventative measures.

    b) Researchers only use animals because they are cheaper and easier to work with.

    c) Alternative research could replace animals in medical testing.

    d) Animals can and do suffer when they are used in medical testing.

2. Which sentence best supports Peter Singer's claim that humans are speciesists?

    a) "Today most people who once wondered or doubted whether animals really could have emotions have discovered that animals do indeed have many of the same kind of emotions that humans have."

    b) "The Johns Hopkins Center for Alternatives to Animal Testing has received grants and gifts to sponsor research, and scientific interest in alternatives has produced legislative initiatives."

    c) "Ultimately, the FDA says, testing must progress to the use of an animal—not using animals for testing would put humans at unreasonable risk."

    d) "The most important reason to consider animals' interests, he says, is that like humans, animals can and do suffer."

Check your answers. Were you correct?

1. d) is the best answer. From the passage, we learned that people who oppose medical testing on animals believe the practice is cruel and causes pain. Darwin's claim that animals feel primary emotions would lead one to believe that they could experience pain and suffering during testing.

2. c) is the best answer. Although the U.S. Food and Drug Administration (FDA) notes that procedures that could replace animals are still in development, they would be unwilling to consider products for humans that had not been tested on other animals first, since it would put humans at risk. This is an example of speciesism, putting the interests of one species above those of other species.

What do you think so far? Is your understanding, analysis, and evaluation of the passage taking shape? Did you return to the passage and find evidence to support your responses? Did your answers match the evidence? Are you comfortable preparing a quick self-evaluation, like the T-chart on pages 21 and 22, to help you organize your ideas about the claims presented and to decide if the reasoning provided is valid, relevant, and sufficient? Once you've done this, you'll be better able to evaluate the argument. Talk through your ideas or jot them down. You can then check your ideas against the expert reader's response.

A Quick Check Self-Evaluation

Argument: Animals Should Not Be Used for Medical Testing

Claim	Valid, Relevant, Sufficient Reasoning
Money spent on experiments using animals could be better spent on preventative measures.	Changing the conditions that lead to a disease is probably better in the long run. Preventative measures might save many more lives.
Researchers only use animals because they are cheaper and easier to work with.	Researchers choose species less for their similarity to humans and more because of lower costs, ease of working with animals, and familiarity.
Alternatives research could replace animals in medical testing.	Development of step-by-step processes could eliminate the need to use animals.

Johns Hopkins Center for Alternatives to Animal Testing has received grants and gifts to sponsor research, and there have been some legislative initiatives. Researchers must find alternatives that work. Procedures are still in development and not ready to try.

The U.S. Food and Drug Administration says not testing on animals puts humans at unreasonable risk. The National Association for Biomedical Research contends there is no substitute for the study of living animals. |
| Animals can and do suffer when they are used in medical testing. | The study of animal minds shows that animals have many of the same emotions as humans.

Charles Darwin wrote that animals can feel fear, disgust, anger, surprise, sadness, and happiness.

Research shows that humans and many other species have limbic systems in the brain that produce six primary emotions. |

Expert Reader's Comments to Claims and Reasoning: I'm having some difficulty with the validity of the reasoning to support several of the claims for this argument. As I evaluate, I don't find that much of the reasoning for the first three claims fulfills the burden of proof and that the reasoning seems based on possibilities and generalizations rather than facts. The final claim and the supporting reasoning, however, seem worth consideration.

Conclusion

How well have you grasped the tips and tricks for evaluating an argument and its claims? Based on your performance and self-evaluation, decide if you've mastered the skills or if you'd benefit from another pass through this guided practice before moving on to chapter 4.

CHAPTER 4

EVALUATING THE ARGUMENTS— ANIMAL RIGHTS— WRITTEN RESPONSE

In chapters 2 and 3, we considered two arguments about animals and medical testing. In this chapter, we'll prepare a written response that evaluates the strengths and weaknesses of both arguments. Then we will assess whether each is supported by sound reasoning and sufficient evidence. To do this, we'll need to use details from both passages.

Task: In the two passages, the author presents arguments for and against using animals for medical testing. Using details from both passages, evaluate the strengths and weaknesses of the arguments, assessing whether each is supported by sound reasoning and sufficient evidence.

Possible response: Your response may be different from the expert reader's, as long as your ideas are supported with evidence from the text and you demonstrate careful analytical thinking and reasoning.

The use of animals for medical testing purposes is a controversial topic. Some believe that medical testing and research on animals is essential for keeping humans safe from life-threatening diseases.

The use of animals for the testing of new medicines, vaccines, surgical methods, and safety standards in cosmetic and food products is a topic that is frequently debated.

Others believe that medical testing on animals is cruel and exposes them to unnecessary suffering. Based on the claims and reasonings in the excerpts I've read, I feel the best-supported argument is that animals should be used for medical testing because it is necessary and benefits humans.

Nearly every twentieth-century medical achievement has used animals in some way. These medical achievements have benefitted humans by allowing them to live more disease-free lives. For example, before 1965, hundreds of thousands of people were paralyzed or killed by the polio virus every year. A vaccine was developed using rhesus monkeys

33

as animal hosts to the virus. Although it is estimated that one hundred thousand monkeys were killed to develop these vaccines, polio is now virtually nonexistent in the United States. Likewise, when a previously unknown, fast-moving coronavirus appeared in 2003 and began affecting humans with lung, breathing, and pneumonia problems, scientists were able to recreate the exact disease in monkeys and quickly develop a vaccine, which potentially saved many lives. While some may criticize humans for being speciesists—creatures that put their interests above those of other species—this has allowed humans to adapt and survive.

Animal rights advocates claim that money spent on experiments using animals could be better spent on preventative measures that might save lives, yet the excerpts provided no solid facts to support this claim. Advocates also suggest that researchers only use animals because they are easier to work with and because they have more familiarity with animals than animal-free alternatives. In fact, although some research facilities have received grants to conduct research into alternative options, no viable options have yet been found. Additionally, the U.S. Food and Drug Administration has indicated that testing must eventually be done on animals prior to humans in order to avoid unreasonable risk to humans. This would indicate that even if animal-free testing options can be developed, medicines, vaccines, and products must still be tested on animals prior to their introduction to humans.

Although there are studies that indicate some animals can feel emotions like fear, surprise and sadness, which might indicate that animal testing causes animals pain, there are federal and state laws and regulations that researchers must follow requiring adequate food and shelter for animals used in medical testing. Many researchers feel that animals deserve to be treated with respect and do them no more harm than is necessary to preserve and support human life.

Nearly every twentieth-century medical achievement has been tested on animals before being tried on humans.

While the use of animals in medical testing can be debated, it is clear that animals should continue to be used for medical testing because it is necessary and benefits humans.

How well did you do? Even if your response was different from the expert reader's, did you apply the tips and tricks in a similar way? Were you able to evaluate the arguments and determine if the claims and reasoning were valid, relevant, and sufficient? If so, you're ready to explore another argument with an expert reader in the next chapter.

CHAPTER 5

EVALUATING AN ARGUMENT— ONE SIDE: IMMIGRATION— EXPERT READER MODEL

Let's see how the tips and tricks for evaluating an argument and its claims could apply to another passage. As before, you'll follow as an expert reader tackles multiple-choice questions and evaluates the claims and reasoning.

⚡ EXPERT READER:

As I learned earlier, I know a debate is a form of argument where there may be opposing views. This passage covers immigration, a complicated topic that is in the news a lot. The multiple headings in the excerpt will clue me in to critical topics. Also, the reader's note will likely give me further insights into immigration.

🏃 An Excerpt from:
Debating the Issues: Immigration
by Ruth Bjorklund

__Note:__ Although immigrant workers played a vital role in the development of the nation, in light of new technology and changes in the global economy, many now say that immigration is no longer a benefit to society and in fact stands in the way of American growth and prosperity.

One Side: Immigration Is No Longer Needed in the United States 🪜

Jobs and Wages

Until the twentieth century, the U.S. economy needed unskilled laborers for agriculture and other labor-intensive jobs such as working on railroad, highway, and other construction projects, in mines and mills, and on assembly lines. The more the country became industrialized, the more factories needed workers. By the middle of the twentieth century, industry grew more technically advanced, and businesses developed a need for a better trained, more highly skilled labor force. 🔍

In 2000, 69% of all adult immigrants had no profession, vocational skill, or job. More than a third of adult immigrants had not graduated from high school. As demand for unskilled labor decreases, competition between immigrant workers and low-wage native-born workers is intensified. Employers not only pay undocumented immigrants (individuals who provide false information about their identity) less money, they deny them most employee benefits such as health insurance. This policy keeps profits high and wages low, and the competition for jobs leads to a reduction in wages and benefits for native-born citizens. 🖊️

🪜 EXPERT READER:

🪜 The note describes the historical context of our nation's need for immigrant workers. This is immediately followed by the argument's premise: Immigration is no longer needed. This is an interesting assertion. Although I may have personal feelings on this topic, I will put them aside.

🔍 The author is building a case in support of the argument by first describing the economic changes in our country and linking this to the changing skills needed among the workforce. The need for skilled workers has replaced the need for unskilled workers. Let's see where this assertion goes.

🖊️ In this paragraph, the author clarifies that changing labor demands impact the issue of immigration by "intensifying" the competition between immigrant workers and low-wage native-born workers. Another issue that seems to impact job competition is the practice of hiring undocumented immigrants. I'll monitor this issue.

In the economic downturn beginning in the last decade, manufacturers, using automated machinery, and other efficient and new technologies, have cut countless low-wage jobs. Manufacturers are also building factories in foreign countries and taking advantage of hiring workers in those countries that can produce goods more cheaply. In 1950 the share of manufacturing jobs in the U.S. was at 33 percent. As of 2010, it had fallen to less than 10 percent.

🗫 EXPERT READER:

Automation and other improved technology in manufacturing has contributed to the decline in unskilled jobs. This seems like a double-edged sword, as well as a matter that further complicates the issue of immigration, jobs, and wages. I'll have to be sure the claims align with this complex argument.

The call for reform in immigration policy is a national issue that sparks much debate and argument.

Health Care Costs

Immigrant families depending on income from low-wage jobs are not as likely as native-born citizens to carry health insurance. Only when people become seriously ill or injured do they seek care, generally from a public clinic or a hospital emergency room. These costs are very expensive, and the burden of payment falls to the government and the taxpayers. A 2006 Census Bureau report stated that 43.8 percent of noncitizens are uninsured, compared with 12.7 percent of native-born citizens.

> ### 📖 EXPERT READER:
>
> In this paragraph, the assertion is that some health care costs for a larger portion of immigrant families may fall to the government and taxpayers. The statistics may support this but we don't have information on actual health care claims.

Education System

Immigrants impact the education system, and many believe that native-born citizens are penalized. In communities where immigration is high, the cost of educating immigrant children who do not speak English is also high. Many classrooms in heavily Latino neighborhoods are taught in both Spanish and English; teachers who are fluent in two languages are paid higher salaries. A Federation for American Immigration Reform (FAIR) report estimates that, depending on class size, it costs $300 to $900 per year per student to provide dual language classes.

> ### 📖 EXPERT READER:
>
> I'm unclear what the author means by the use of the word "penalized." Also, I wonder how the per student fee was calculated by FAIR. Although there are likely costs associated with dual language instruction, I'm not sure this section addresses the matter convincingly.

Professional Wage Earners

In the past two decades, middle-class workers and professional high-wage workers have also been adversely affected by immigrant competition, in particular, because of a visa program known as H-1B. This program allows highly trained foreign workers with particular skills (usually of a high-tech nature) to be employed by American companies in the United States when no qualified native-born citizens are available. The employer is required to hire the H-1B visa holder at prevailing wages—in other words, at the same wage that would be paid to a U.S. citizen in the same job, but there have been many abuses to the system. Many employers find ways to hire professionals from other countries and pay them lower wages than an American employee would receive. In response to widespread complaints, Congress reduced the size of the H-1B program, though it permitted so many exemptions that displaced American professionals continued to be very angry.

EXPERT READER:

The point of view presented here parallels concerns over "immigrant competition" presented earlier for the low-skilled workers. I was unaware of this visa program and its effects on professional wage earners.

Initially, the H1-B program seemed to justify and legitimize the employment of highly skilled immigrant workers. Yet abusive business practices seem to be causing the "adverse" issues for professional workers.

Illegal Immigration

For many people, a big part of any discussion about immigration centers on illegal (undocumented) immigration. Data suggest that there are approximately 12 million illegal immigrants living in the United States, yet it is difficult to be accurate about these numbers. The Center for Immigration Studies (CSI) says that illegal immigrants help and encourage their friends and family members to also enter the country illegally, a situation that increases the drag on wages and the competition with legal citizens for jobs. ⚠

Americans also have concerns about illegal immigrants and law enforcement. According to the Department of Homeland Security *Yearbook of Immigration Statistics*, more than 200,000 illegal aliens were imprisoned in 2008 for committing crimes such as theft, burglary, assault, and murder, and many of them were later deported. The attacks on the World Trade Center in New York City in 1993 and 2001 were largely perpetrated by persons in the country illegally. 🗨

📖 EXPERT READER:

⚠ I know it's important to weigh all claims carefully instead of being swayed in a direction. I'm unsure how to weigh the concerns about illegal immigration in terms of the larger scope of the topic—the need for immigration. Are these two separate matters? I appreciate that it's hard to separate them, yet I must exercise some caution here.

🗨 I recognize the importance of the safety and security of our nation. The statistics provided are alarming. I will have to carefully review the claims and evidence to evaluate the author's argument.

Mini Assessment

Let's see how the expert reader tackles some multiple-choice questions on this passage. Notice that in some cases, more than one answer may be considered correct. It is important to use evidence to build a case for the best answer. Returning to the passage will be helpful.

1. The author claims that competition between immigrant workers and low-wage native-born workers is intensified because of the declining demand for unskilled labor. Which sentence does *not* support this claim?

a) "As of 2010, [manufacturing jobs] had fallen to less than 10 percent."

b) "In the economic downturn beginning in the last decade,

manufacturers, using automated machinery, and other efficient and new technologies, have cut countless low-wage jobs."

c) "In the past two decades, middle-class workers and professional high-wage workers have also been adversely affected by immigrant competition."

d) "By the middle of the twentieth century, industry grew more technically advanced, and businesses developed a need for a better trained, more highly skilled labor force."

2. Which statement is most strongly supported by evidence in the passage?

a) Issues arising from illegal immigration adversely affect other challenges the nation faces surrounding immigration.

b) Health insurance coverage is costly and prohibitive for unskilled workers, including immigrant families.

c) Manufacturing jobs in the United States have decreased largely because factories are being built in foreign countries where goods can be produced more cheaply.

d) The cost of providing dual language instruction is three times greater than providing single language instruction.

Check your answers. Were you correct?

1. c) is the best answer. Although none of the statements support the idea of heightened competition, several provide reasons explaining the decline in low-wage, unskilled jobs. These include answers a), b), and d). Therefore the best answer is c). It does not explain reasons for the decline in low-wage unskilled jobs.

2. a) is the best answer. Although this issue is not explicitly stated in the article, the author provides multiple pieces of strong evidence that support the idea that difficulties stem from illegal immigration. Answers b) and c) are discussed in the passage, yet in comparison to choice a) are not as strong. Answer d) is inaccurate.

Expert Reader: I'm satisfied with my responses. In all cases, I returned to the text to check possible answers against evidence. I'm confident I can support my answers. Now I'm ready to organize my thoughts into a T-chart. This will help me refine my ideas about the claims—are they valid, relevant, and sufficient? Once I've determine this, I can better evaluate the argument.

A Quick Check Self-Evaluation

Argument: Immigration Is No Longer Needed

It is no longer a benefit to society and stands in the way of American growth and prosperity.

Claim	Valid, Relevant, and Sufficient Reasoning
Jobs and wages: Low-wage jobs are declining. As demand for unskilled labor decreases, competition between immigrant workers and low-wage native-born workers is intensified.	The U.S. economy has shifted and no longer needs unskilled labor. There are a limited number of unskilled jobs, heightening the competition for them. In 1950 the share of manufacturing jobs in the United States was at 33 percent. Less than a decade ago it was below 10 percent. Some businesses hire undocumented immigrants, resulting in practices that negatively impact native citizens.
Health care costs and education system: Immigrant families may burden government and taxpayers with health care costs and educational expenses.	Immigrant families earning income from low-wage jobs are not as likely as native-born citizens to carry health insurance. According to Census data, 43.8 percent of noncitizens are uninsured, compared with 12.7 percent of native-born citizens. Payment of health care costs burdens the government and taxpayers. Education costs for immigrant children who do not speak English is high, with costs of $300 to $900 per year per student for dual language classes.

Professional wage earners: Immigrant competition for highly trained, high-tech positions adversely affects American professionals.	The H-1B visa allows employment for highly trained foreign workers by American companies at prevailing wages when no qualified native-born citizens are available. Employers find ways to hire foreign-born professionals and pay them lower wages than American employees.
Illegal immigration: Illegal immigrants help and encourage their friends and family members to also enter the country illegally. Americans have concerns about illegal immigrants and law enforcement.	Illegal immigration increases the drag on wages and the competition with legal citizens for jobs. More than two hundred thousand illegal aliens were imprisoned and later deported in 2008 for committing crimes. The attacks on the World Trade Center were largely perpetrated by persons in the country illegally.

Expert Reader's Comments to Claims and Reasoning: After evaluating my T-chart, I have doubts about the validity of some of the claims. Increased costs for health care and education are suggested, yet the data provided to support this seems incomplete or misaligned. There may also be shortfalls with claims and reasoning used in discussions on professional wage earners. Some of the difficulties with the H-1B visa are a result of abusive business practices, which is a problem that seems to complicate others on immigration. The same is true for problems that stem from illegal immigration, which contribute to many of the complaints about job competition and crime. Although these matters are important, I wonder if these abusive practices shouldn't be considered separately.

Conclusion

How well do you feel you understand the expert reader's use of the tips and tricks for evaluating an argument and its claims? You can move on to the guided practice in the next chapter or take another pass through the expert reader's model.

CHAPTER 6

EVALUATING AN ARGUMENT—THE OTHER SIDE: IMMIGRATION—GUIDED PRACTICE

Directions: Now it's time for you to apply the tips and tricks in your close reading of a passage. The practice prompt icons will guide you. Check to see if your responses to the prompts match the possible responses provided.

An Excerpt from:
Debating the Issues: Immigration
by Ruth Bjorklund

Note: Many think that America's strength and success has come from being a nation of immigrants. Many immigrants who have come to America have had considerable drive and ambition. Rejecting the status quo in their

🖥 GUIDED PRACTICE PROMPT:

How can jump-start clues help you? Possible response: The structure of this passage is similar to the one in the earlier chapter. The note will give context for the argument, and the headings and subheadings will guide my thinking. This passage will offer claims to support the position that immigration is vital.

native countries, they sought a life that offered freedom, prosperity, and a better chance of success and equality for their children. One has only to look at the richness of American life to see their influences. 🔍

GUIDED PRACTICE PROMPT:

🔍 Can you identify the author's point of view or perspective? Possible response: The author presents a positive, almost charming description of immigration. Positive descriptions like "considerable drive and ambition" and words like "richness" further persuade readers. They create appeal for the argument that immigration is vital to the United States.

▤ How can you use text structures to help establish the argument? Possible response: The author begins this section on the economy by addressing claims from an opposing side and then refuting them—proving them false. This is a strong approach that allows me to weigh all claims carefully. Still, I'll have to evaluate the data used to refute the opposite claim.

🗨 What are you thinking? Possible response: The quote from Daniel Griswold highlights a positive outcome. It offsets the negative problems related to the low-skilled immigrant workforce. Encouraging native-born students and adults to seek further education and job skills is an interesting counterclaim. Still, I would want to explore this idea a bit more.

The Other Side: Immigration Is Vital to the United States Economy

People who wish to limit immigration often claim that immigrants take jobs away from native-born citizens and negatively impact the lives of native-born low-wage earners. However, those who favor immigration point to data and reports from numerous sources that reject those claims. ▤ Writing in the *Bulletin for Free Trade*, Daniel Griswold offered a claim that while low-skilled, foreign-born workers may affect wages, the immigrant workers add more to the economy than they take in return. "The arrival of low-skilled, foreign-born workers in the labor force increases the incentives for younger native-born American to stay in school and for older workers to upgrade their skills" and advance upwardly in the labor force. Thus, he says, they do not compete with foreign-born workers. 🗨 John Gay, of the American Hotel and Lodging Association, holds a similar belief, as quoted in *USA Today*: "There are places in this country where we wouldn't survive without immigrants....The trend is to push our own children into college to be rocket scientists or computer programmers. But who is going to do these hard jobs that we have?" ⚠ In a recent *Wall Street Journal* article, Tamar Jacoby, president of Immigration Works USA, said that Americans are growing more educated. She says only 10 percent of native-born males drop out of high school to look for unskilled work, compared with 50 percent in 1960. Fewer native-born workers apply for low-wage jobs when they have lost better-paying jobs. Native-born workers are also much less likely to uproot themselves and move elsewhere to look for work. Immigrant low-wage workers, on the other hand, are more flexible and will travel anywhere for work; for example, they seek jobs in chicken-processing factories in Arkansas and meatpacking plants in Kansas,

Native-born workers tend to "cluster at the middle rungs of the economic ladder," and that immigrants are more likely found at the lower and upper rungs. "By and large," she writes, "newcomers complement rather than compete with those already here."

💻 GUIDED PRACTICE PROMPT:

⚠ Are you safeguarding your thinking against common pitfalls? Possible response: This author uses opinions and stirring descriptive passages. She also gives supportive facts. The evidence by John Gay contains highly charged personal opinion. I hope there is other evidence to support it.

💬 What are you thinking? Possible response: Here, the evidence supplied by Tamar Jacoby partly supports John Gay's opinion. The collection of evidence suggests that unskilled, low-wage jobs are undesirable to the U.S. workforce. They may be difficult to fill without the immigrant workforce.

📝 Do you notice the author's craft and structure? Possible response: The author provides several claims to cast doubt on the negative effects of immigration on native-born workers and the economy. The claims also support immigration as a prompt for workers to improve and to fill "hard" jobs that do not attract native workers and that serve as a complement to the U.S. workforce.

Taxes and Government Benefits

Many of those opposed to immigration claim that immigrants take more from the government than they give back. Some refute this claim. One representative from the Social Security Administration (SSA) said that immigration helps the system "remain solvent" and relies on immigrants' contributions to Social Security taxes. Retirees benefit from the taxes that immigrant workers contribute. The National Research Council reports that the nation's 34 million immigrants pay more in taxes than they consume in public services and benefits. Most of them work and pay federal, state, and local taxes. Furthermore, the report has found that many immigrants, once near retirement age, return to their home countries and do not ever claim American Social Security or Medicare benefits.

GUIDED PRACTICE PROMPT:

Do you notice the author's craft and structure? Possible response: These arguments dispute claims from the first one. Additionally, we learn that many immigrants do not claim benefits. I didn't know this.

What are you thinking? Possible response: This data appears to dispute earlier claims. Yet I question whether it addresses crime statistics about illegal aliens. This matter was raised in the earlier passage. The quotes from authorities that rely on testimony and Census data suggest the data is valid. But is it relevant?

Crime Statistics

Immigration detractors assert that there is a high cost of crime associated with immigrants. In testimony before Congress in 2007, Professor Anne Piehl of Rutgers University used census data to support her claim that immigrants are imprisoned for crimes at one-fifth the rate of native-born citizens. Professor Ruben Rumbaut of the University of California also used Census data to show that immigrants without high school diplomas had an incarceration rate that was one-fourth that of native-born high school graduates and one-seventh that of native-born citizens who did not graduate from high school.

Professional Immigrant Workers

About one in three immigrants has a college degree, and among them, 42 percent hold master's, professional, or doctorate degrees compared with 36 percent of college-educate, native-born citizens. These individuals have made major contributions to America's success, especially in mathematics, science, medicine, and high technology. A recent Duke University study showed that in the past decade, immigrants founded 25 percent of all new American engineering and technology companies. Immigrants were also listed as inventors or co inventors of 24 percent of all patents in 2006.

Illegal Immigration

Illegal immigration is a problem in this country and a dilemma for politicians and the public alike. Illegal immigrants live a life "in the shadows," and while they work and support their families, in many states they are ineligible for the rights and benefits available to legal residents and citizens.

GUIDED PRACTICE PROMPT:

What are you thinking? Possible response: I'm surprised at this data only because it was not raised in the first passage. These contributions are extremely valuable to the nation.

Have you used text structure to explore support for a claim? Possible response: There is very little specifically addressing illegal immigration. I'm really beginning to see how data can be used to both support and contest important matters. Even an absence of information is noteworthy when evaluating an argument. I appreciate the importance of giving careful thought to the validity of claims and supporting evidence.

Government Services and the Economy

Immigrant workers stimulate the economy in many ways. According to the Selig Center for Economic Growth at the University of Georgia, in 2008 foreign-born consumers purchased more than 14 percent of the nation's goods and services, and that total reached $1.5 trillion. This provided state and local governments with sales

🖥 GUIDED PRACTICE PROMPT:

📖 Have you used text structure to help identify claims throughout the passage? Possible response: In this passage, the author included some statements that reflected opinion or generalizations, yet claims were also supported by facts and what seems to be sound data. In some cases, however, I would have to explore some of the sources, such as "A National Academy of Sciences study," a bit more to ensure the reliability of the data.

tax income. A National Academy of Sciences study found that an average immigrant and his or her children will pay $80,000 more in taxes than they ever would collect in government services. For immigrants with high-wage professions, the taxes they pay over the period of their careers amount to $20,000 or more. 📖

Mini Assessment

Let's see how you do on some multiple-choice questions for the passage. Even though more than one answer may seem correct, it's important to identify the best response.

1. Read this sentence from the passage: "Native born workers, on the other hand, are more flexible and will travel anywhere for work." Why does the author include this sentence?

a) To support the statement that "newcomers complement rather than compete with those already here."

b) To establish the fact that immigrant workers add more to the economy than they take in return.

c) To make sure readers understand the magnitude of the claim that many immigrants who have come to America have had considerable drive and ambition.

d) To increase her believability as an expert on flexible work trends.

2. Which sentence best supports the claim that professional immigrant workers have made major contributions to America's success, especially in mathematics, science, medicine, and high technology?

> **a)** The immigrant workers add more to the economy than they take in return.
>
> **b)** In a year-long study, immigrants founded 25 percent of all new American engineering and technology companies.
>
> **c)** Immigrant low-wage workers are more flexible and will travel anywhere for work.
>
> **d)** Many immigrants who have come to America have had considerable drive and ambition.

Check your answers against an expert reader's. Were you correct?

1. a) is the best answer. From the passage, we learned that some people claim that immigrants take jobs away from native-born citizens. This negatively impacts the lives of native-born low-wage earners. Here, the sentence refutes that statement. It shows a difference in job-seeking trends between immigrant and native-born workers, suggesting the trends work together.

2. b) is the best answer. It states that nearly one-quarter of all engineering and technology companies were created by immigrants, which has helped to strengthen America's success in these areas. Although choices a) and d) could also suggest this, b) is a more specific answer. Choice c) does not answer the question.

What do you think so far? Did you return to the passage and find evidence to support your responses? Did your answers square with the evidence? Are you comfortable using a quick check self-evaluation graphic organizer, like a T-chart? This will help you organize your ideas about the claims and decide if the reasoning is valid, relevant, and sufficient. Either talk through your T-chart or note your thoughts on a piece of paper. You can then compare your ideas to the expert reader's response.

A Quick Check Self-Evaluation

Argument: Immigration Is Vital to the United States

Claim	Valid, Relevant & Sufficient Reasoning
Economy: Immigrants do not take jobs from or negatively impact native-born low-wage earners.	Low-skilled, foreign-born workers increase incentives for Americans to stay in school/upgrade skills. Some jobs are hard and require a willingness to relocate. Native-born workers "cluster at the middle rungs of the economic ladder" and immigrants are more likely found at lower and upper levels.
Taxes and government benefits: Immigrants contribute to and help government more than they take from it. Immigrants stimulate the economy.	Immigration helps keep some government programs like Social Security solvent. The nation's thirty-four million immigrants pay more in taxes than they consume in benefits. Fourteen percent of the nation's goods were purchased by foreign-born consumers and they contribute a good amount to taxes.
Crime: Immigrants come to America to pursue opportunity and do not want to compromise this by breaking laws.	Immigrants are imprisoned at one-fifth the rate of natives. Immigrants without high school diplomas had an incarceration rate one-fourth that of native-born high school graduates and one-seventh that of native-born citizens who did not graduate from high school.
Professional wage earners: Professional immigrant workers have contributed to America's success.	Twenty-five percent of all new American engineering/technology companies were founded by immigrants. Immigrants invented or coinvented 24 percent of all patents in a year-long study.
Illegal immigration: Illegal immigrants live in the shadows.	Some illegal immigrants are ineligible for the rights and benefits available to legal residents and citizens.

Expert Reader's Comments to Claims and Reasoning: After evaluating my T-chart, I feel the argument that immigration is vital to the economy is well supported. The author uses a strong line of claims and reasoning. I was concerned that the passage had several opinions and emotional statements. However, facts and evidence were also used. The claims seem valid as they are supported by statements from credible authorities, with data from reliable sources. The claims are also relevant and sufficient as they offset arguments from immigrant detractors and *mostly* support new claims about the vitality of immigration.

Conclusion

How well have you grasped the tips and tricks for evaluating an argument and its claims? Based on your performance and self-evaluation, decide if you've mastered the skills. If not, you can pass through this guided practice again before moving on to chapter 7.

EVALUATING THE ARGUMENTS— IMMIGRATION—WRITTEN RESPONSE

In chapters 4 and 5, you had an opportunity to consider two arguments about immigration. In this chapter, you'll prepare a written response that evaluates the strengths and weaknesses of both arguments. You will also assess whether each argument is supported by sound reasoning and sufficient evidence.

Task: In the two passages, the author presents arguments for and against the need for and vitality of immigration in the United States. Using specific details from both passages, evaluate the strengths and weaknesses of the arguments, assessing whether each is supported by sound reasoning and sufficient evidence.

Possible Response: Your response may be different from the expert reader's. That's OK, as long as you've supported your ideas with evidence from the text. You should also show careful analytical thinking and reasoning.

Most people would agree that the United States grew and prospered as a result of the hard work and contributions of immigrants. Today, however, some argue whether or not the benefits remain. Based on the claims and reasoning in the excerpts I have read, I feel that the argument that immigration is still needed in the United States is best supported.

One criticism against immigration is that foreign-born workers take jobs away from native citizens. Tamar Jacoby, president of Immigration Works USA, offers another view, that "newcomers complement rather than compete with those already here." Low-wage, difficult, and regionally based jobs have not often been favored by native-born workers. Instead, they cluster in mid-level jobs. Despite correct claims that there are fewer low-wage manufacturing jobs, there is little proof that native-born workers compete to fill them. It seems the real complaints immigration opponents have on work-related matters are over the abusive employment practices of hiring undocumented immigrants.

Related issues that fuel debate on immigration are practices surrounding the professional workforce. Immigration opponents feel this group of U.S. workers is also at a disadvantage. They claim the H-1B visa creates unfair competition for high-tech positions. However, it appears that the real problem is that U.S. employers use the visa program unfairly. This reduces opportunities for American professionals. The problem is caused by employers, not workers. Interestingly, those who favor immigration believe that professional immigrant workers have made major contributions to America's success. Ample evidence backs this up. According to a year-long study, 25 percent of all new American engineering and technology companies were founded by immigrants. Also, immigrants were listed as inventors or coinventors of 24 percent of all patents. The contribution of these foreign-born professionals seems clear.

Another issue that upsets those against immigration is extra costs they link to the immigrant population. This includes health care, education, and other public service costs. U.S. Census data confirms that many more immigrant families are uninsured compared to native-born citizens. However, the passage did not supply how those costs apply only to uninsured immigrant families. Arguments surrounding additional education costs and other service costs are also weakened by a lack of reliable support. Immigration supporters, on the other hand, present well-supported claims that prove the positive role immigrants play as consumers and tax payers.

While these opposing views on immigration raise difficult questions, the challenges are further complicated by problems that arise from illegal immigration and the questionable and abusive employment practices that surround it. Those against immigration claim employers who hire undocumented immigrants create workforce problems. Another problem linked to illegal immigration is crime and even terrorism. Still, immigration supporters argue that immigrants come to America to "pursue opportunity and do not want to compromise this by breaking laws."

Although there is some validity to the arguments made by those who believe immigration is no longer needed, I believe that supporters of immigration not only made a stronger case for their position but also successfully argued against the major issues raised by those who oppose it. Additionally, those who find fault with immigration mostly target their criticism at *illegal* immigration and the abusive business practices surrounding it.

Conclusion

How well have you grasped the tips and tricks to evaluate an argument and its claims? Based on your performance and self-evaluation, decide if you've mastered the skills or if you would like to take another pass through this guided practice. Congratulations if you're ready to move on!

A New Expert Reader!

Now that you've mastered how to use the tips and tricks for evaluating an argument and its claims, you're on your way to becoming an expert reader! Continue to practice with different types of informational texts.

ANALYZE To carefully examine, inspect, and consider a text in order to fully understand it.

ARGUMENT A view or position that someone takes and supports through a line of reasoning and claims.

CENTRAL IDEA The key concept or message being expressed.

CLAIM An assertion or statement.

CLOSE READING The deep, analytical reading of a brief passage of text in which the reader constructs meaning based on author intention and text evidence. The close reading of a text enables readers to gain insights that exceed a cursory reading.

DELINEATE To define or explain.

DISTRACTOR Anything that steers a reader away from the text evidence and weakens or misguides analysis.

EVALUATE To appraise or assess.

EVIDENCE Information from the text that a reader uses to prove a position, conclusion, inference, or big idea.

FIX-UP STRATEGY Common technique used when meaning is lost.

GENRE A system used to classify types or kinds of writing.

INFORMATIONAL TEXT A type of nonfiction text, such as articles, essays, opinion piece, memoirs, and historical, scientific, technical, or economic accounts, that is written to give facts or inform about a topic.

POINT OF VIEW The perspective, or position, of the person relaying information.

RELEVANT Closely connected or appropriate to the matter at hand.

SUFFICIENT Enough; an adequate amount.

TEXT FEATURE Any of the variety of tools used to organize text and to give readers more information about the text.

TEXT STRUCTURE The logical arrangement and organization of ideas in a text using sentences, lines, paragraphs, stanzas, or sections.

TONE The writer's communication of an overall feeling or attitude about a book's subject, content, or topic.

VALID Having a sound basis in logic or fact.

FOR MORE INFORMATION

Council of Chief State School Officers
One Massachusetts Avenue NW
Suite 700
Washington, DC 20001-1431
(202) 336-7000
Website: http://www.ccsso.org
The Common Core State Standards Initiative is a state-led effort coordinated
by the National Governors Association Center for Best Practices (NGA
Center) and the Council of Chief State School Officers (CCSSO).

National Governors Association
Hall of the States
444 North Capitol Street, Suite 267
Washington, DC 20001-1512
(202) 624-5300
Website: http://www.nga.org
The National Governors Association and the Council of Chief State School
Officers go together—both organizations were responsible for the creation
of the Common Core State Standards so they share the description provided.

National Parent Teacher Association
12250 North Pitt Street
Alexandria, VA 22314
(703) 518-1200
Website: http://www.pta.org
The National PTA enthusiastically supports the adoption and implementation
by all states of the Common Core State Standards.

New York State Education Department
89 Washington Avenue
Albany, NY 12234
(518) 474-3852
Website: http://www.engageny.org
EngageNY.org is developed and maintained by the New York State Education
   Department. This is the official website for current materials and
   resources related to the implementation of the New York State P–12
   Common Core Learning Standards.

Partnership for Assessment of Readiness for College and Careers
1400 16th Street NW, Suite 510
Washington, DC 20036
(202) 745-2311
Website: http://www.parcconline.org
The Partnership for Assessment of Readiness for College and Careers is a consor-
   tium of eighteen states plus the District of Columbia and the U.S. Virgin
   Islands working together to develop a common set of K–12 assessments in
   English and math.

U.S. Department of Education
Department of Education Building
400 Maryland Avenue SW
Washington, DC 20202
(800) 872-5327
Website: http://www.ed.gov
Nearly every state now has adopted the Common Core State Standards.
   The federal government has supported this state-led effort by helping

to ensure that higher standards are being implemented for all students and that educators are being supported in transitioning to new standards.

Websites

Because of the changing nature of Internet links, Rosen Publishing has developed an online list of websites related to the subject of this book. This site is updated regularly. Please use this link to access the list:

http://www.rosenlinks.com/CCRGR/Argu

Beers, Kylene, and Robert E. Probst. *Notice & Note: Strategies for Close Reading*. Portsmouth, NH: Heinemann, 2013.

Bjorklund, Ruth. *Debating the Issues: Immigration*. Tarrytown, NY: Marshall Cavendish Benchmark, 2011.

Fountas, Irene C., and Gay Su Pinnell. *Genre Study: Teaching with Fiction and Nonfiction Books*. Portsmouth, NH: Heinemann, 2012.

Mack, Gail. *Debating the Issues: Animal Rights*. Tarrytown, NY: Marshall Cavendish Benchmark, 2011.

INDEX

A

Anchor Standard 8, 6
arguments, delineating and evaluating, 6
   expert reader models, 15–22, 36–44
   guided practices, 23–31, 45¬–53
   self-evaluations for, 13
   skills needed, 8–10
   written responses, 32–35, 54–56
author credibility, 11

C

close reading, about, 6
College and Career Readiness Anchor
   Standards, 5
Common Core Reading Standards,
   about, 5, 6
craft and text structure, using, 11–12

D

Debating the Issues: Animal Rights,
   excerpts from, 15–19, 23–27
   mini assessments of, 20–21, 28–29
   quick check self-evaluations, 21–22,
   29–31
   written response, 32–35
Debating the Issues: Immigration,
   excerpts from, 36–41

   mini assessments of, 41–43
   quick check self-evaluations, 43–44
   written response, 54–56

G

guided practice, described, 6–7

I

inferences, making, 10
inside voice, tuning in to, 12–13

J

jump-start clues, launching, 10

P

pitfalls, avoiding common, 13–14
point of view/perspective, identifying
   and monitoring, 11

R

reading comprehension skills, 6

T

text analysis tips and tricks, 10–14
text structure, using to find central idea
   or argument, 10–11

About the Authors

Sandra K. Athans is a national board-certified practicing classroom teacher with fifteen years of experience teaching reading and writing at the elementary level. She is the author of several teacher-practitioner books on literacy including *Quality Comprehension* and *Fun-tastic Activities for Differentiating Comprehension Instruction*, both published by the International Reading Association. Athans has presented her research at the International Reading Association, the National Council of Teachers of English Conferences, and the New York State Reading Association Conferences. Her contributions have appeared in well-known literacy works including *The Literacy Leadership Handbook* and *Strategic Writing Mini-Lessons*. She is also a children's book writer and specializes in high-interest, photo-informational books published with Millbrook Press.

Athans earned a B.A. in English from the University of Michigan, an M.A. in elementary education from Manhattanville College, and an M.S. in literacy (birth through grade 6) from Le Moyne College. She is also certified to teach secondary English. In addition to teaching in the classroom, she is an adjunct professor at Le Moyne College and provides instruction in graduate-level literacy classes. She was named an outstanding elementary social studies educator by the Central New York Council for the Social Studies. Athans serves on various ELA leadership networks and collaborates with educators nationwide to address the challenges of the Common Core Standards. The Tips and Tricks series is among several Common Core resources she has authored for Rosen Publishing.

Robin W. Parente is a practicing reading specialist and classroom teacher with over fifteen years of experience teaching reading and writing at the elementary level. She also serves as the elementary ELA coordinator for a medium-sized district in central New York, working with classroom teachers to implement best literacy practices in the classroom. Parente earned a B.S. in elementary education and an M.S. in education/literacy from the State University of New York at Oswego. She is a certified reading specialist (PK through 12) and elementary classroom teacher and has served on various ELA leadership networks to collaborate with educators to address the challenges of the Common Core Standards. The Tips and Tricks series is among several Common Core resources she has authored for Rosen Publishing.

Photo Credits